H

Hand Job

❖

An Insider's Look Into The Modeling Business

by
Mike Ramsey

iUniverse, Inc.
New York Lincoln Shanghai

Hand Job
An Insider's Look Into The Modeling Business

iUniverse, Inc.

For information address:
iUniverse, Inc.
2021 Pine Lake Road, Suite 100
Lincoln, NE 68512
www.iuniverse.com

ISBN: 0-595-30894-5

Printed in the United States of America

Contents

How-to Section Of The Book

From the author

I've got a little secret to tell you. That good-looking guy, wearing the designer suit in the ad in the Sunday paper, may have been the same guy who was your waiter at your favorite restaurant last Saturday night.

Surprised? You shouldn't be. In any given major market, only about 2 or 3% of all people who call themselves models, actually make a living at modeling. Not many will admit it, but 90% of all aspiring models never make enough money on actual paying jobs, to pay for the expenses necessary just to call themselves a model.

I actually knew guys who would rent couches from other models for $50 or $100 per month, or sleep in their car and shower at the gym. They kept all of their clothes in their car. Since several local nightclubs had made arrangements for models at our agency to get in without a cover charge, they would visit during happy hour, order water to drink, and then stuff themselves at the free buffet for their one meal of the day. I even knew one guy who spent his time in Milan, Italy sleeping in a hotel lobby and on park benches. Sounds glamorous, doesn't it?

If they are lucky and actually make it into the business, they may be able to earn hundreds of dollars per month modeling, but spend much more than that on photographs, composite cards, headbooks, and other materials needed for them to be considered professional models. It turns into a fun hobby for most, allowing them to tell everyone that they are models. You probably know someone just like this. Maybe that waiter I mentioned earlier.

Quickly, name as many models as you can. How many of them are still actual working models? Most of the top names we remember may have been considered "supermodels" a decade or more ago, and have long since been replaced by the next generation. It is extremely rare for anyone to make it as a top model, particularly men. Only the most involved industry insiders ever remember the guys' names.

This is one of the reasons why such a big deal is made of the elite few who go on to become household names. I believe that the odds against a new model ever making it to "supermodel" status are higher than a high school athlete making it to All-Star status as a pro.

I was lucky enough to have worked and played with a few of the top models of the '80s, both male and female, and learned a lot about the modeling business. Some of them went on to be stars in TV, movies, and music. Most of us moved on to "real jobs" after going as far as we thought we could go in show biz.

I was extremely fortunate to have been able to make a decent living modeling in the 1980s and early '90s. Certainly a little luck was involved, but it was primarily a combination of decent genetics and a lot of hard work, persistence, and flexibility, that allowed me to figure out how to break into the business.

People still have a very difficult time believing that a camera-shy guy, raised in small towns in Texas, somehow went on to be a model, on covers of magazines, in TV commercials, on radio, and in movies. I think that contrast is what makes the stories so interesting and humorous. Ask anybody in show business, and they will be able to tell you lots of stories about how strange the business is. The perspective of a naïve, small-town Texan makes the stories funnier, I think.

I've been telling my modeling stories to friends and associates for years, and they have often said I should write a book about my experiences. I decided the time was right for the book, for a couple of reasons. First, I hope the story of how I made it into the modeling business is interesting to you and makes you laugh a little. Second, if you or anyone you know is considering getting into modeling, maybe the information in this book will either help you avoid some problems and mistakes, or maybe even decide that modeling is not the right direction to go.

There are far too many stories to include them all, so I have made this book primarily about how various circumstances, some within my control and others outside of my control, caused me to move into the business of specialty modeling, including hands, body parts, runway, and underwear. As I have previously pointed out, it is incredibly hard for a male model to make a full time living. I decided that I would take any opportunities to make a living, and this book tells the story of how a guy who did all of the things necessary to be a fashion model, ended up being known more for his hands and other parts, than for his face.

I chose the title of the book for its double meaning. When my agent would call me with a booking for my hands, he or she would tell me I had a "hand job". That's what we called it. The other meaning of the title relates to how I sometimes felt I was treated as a model. I'll leave it to your imagination.

The names of the people in the stories are real. I have used first names only of people who did not go on to become famous celebrities, just in case they don't want to bring attention to themselves. Celebrities, on the other hand, know that having stories written about them is all part of show biz, and do not expect any such anonymity. All of the stories are true, witnessed by myself, so you will get a pretty good idea of how the business works.

I hope you enjoy the book, and maybe learn a few things. Thanks for reading it.

Mike Ramsey

Introduction

✦

Study Hall, 1974-75

Several students gathered around Ms. Baggett's desk as the bell rang to start class. She had always been the most popular Government teacher, and often had a crowd at her desk before class. Ms. Baggett was young, pretty, and fashionably dressed.

That was usually enough to keep both the male and female students vying for her attention, but today there was a special draw. She had brought the new batch of fashion magazines featuring her favorite former pupil, Jerry Hall. There were several of them, Vogue, Glamour, Harper's Bazaar and others, spread out across her desk, with Jerry's photos prominently displayed.

Jerry had been in Ms. Baggett's class a couple of years earlier. She was a year older then I was, and graduated early to be able to go to Europe and model. She seemed to know that she belonged somewhere other than Mesquite, Texas, and couldn't wait to get out and take on the fashion world. Most of the students at North Mesquite High just thought she was strange. At the time, she wasn't considered one of the good-looking girls. Jerry certainly wasn't the cheerleader type, or homecoming queen, or any of the usual categories where we put the "pretty" girls.

Jerry Hall's 1973 High School photo

There was something different about her. In hindsight, she always knew what she wanted and where she was going. At the time, those who even noticed her just thought she was a little full of herself and a little weird. She was tall and gangly, and her quirky fashion statements stood out starkly against the monochromatic fashion displays of the middle class high school girls.

Today, it's easy to see where she was going, and how none of the rest of us had a clue as to how big a splash she was going to make in the fashion world over the next couple of decades.

But back then, standing around Ms. Baggett's desk, I looked at a completely foreign world. My generic jean and chukka boot fashion sense didn't allow me to understand the significance of Jerry's accomplishment.

Mike's 1974 High School photo

Adding to my lack of ability to appreciate what it meant for her to make it into fashion magazines, was the fact that men simply weren't a part of that world at the time, certainly not real men from Texas. It just didn't register that I would ever find that kind of thing important. I would never have imagined that some-day, I would head in that same direction.

While it took about seven years for circumstances and coincidences to lead me to pursue becoming a model, those images of Jerry always stuck with me. The seed was planted. All that was required was for somebody to water it.

Setting the Stage

"The next awards are for most years of perfect attendance", Mr. McCoy, the Assistant Principal announced at the all-school awards assembly. "The nerd award", was muttered loudly by several kids, with giggles coming from groups scattered across the auditorium.

This was near the end of the assembly, and the natives were restless. While school assemblies were always welcome as a chance to get out of class, teenagers in high school can't sit still for very long. Not only was this award one that almost no self-respecting cool kid would ever try to get, everybody was bored and wanted to go. Things would get more interesting in a minute.

"Four years of perfect attendance", was announced, and a dozen or so students came up. Many of them were moderately popular; athletes, band members, or class officers. It was hard to make it through four years of high school without an unexcused absence, but it was possible, even for fairly normal kids. None of these awards elicited much in the way of catcalls or rude remarks.

"Six years", was next. The crowd of recipients thinned considerably. These were the ones who had made it all the way from 7th grade to 12th without an absence. A handful of students, some with thick glasses, others with "high water" pants, marched up to the stage and received their awards, to the growing rumble of laughs and name rhyming from the crowd.

"Twelve years of perfect attendance", pronounced Mr. McCoy, more loudly than the previous ones. "We have two students who have made it all the way from 1st grade to graduating from High School, without an unexcused absence." "I wonder who these geeks are", I thought to myself, having no clue what my attendance record was. Mr. McCoy announced the first name, a name I cannot remember, and then read the second name, "and Michael Ramsey".

I sat there for what seemed to be minutes, and then jumped up to go to the stage. I had no idea that I was getting an attendance award, "But hey, at least I get to go up on stage and show everybody that I'm not the nerd they think I am". The crowd seemed to disagree, and mixed snickers and guffaws in with their smattering of applause as I walked to the front of the auditorium. I swaggered to the bottom of the steps at stage right, and proceeded to take the steps two and three at a time. I wanted to show the audience that I was a cool guy. This is my big moment.

Keep in mind that I had recently been identified as a "smart kid", graduating seventh in my class of around 500 seniors. I was one of only three kids in Mr. Wagliardo's Computer Math class, where we ran programs in Basic on the Bell Labs computer in New Jersey, over a Teletype machine. I was a prototype computer geek. To put this in historical perspective, Bill Gates had not yet started Microsoft.

Four years of high school, and I was just beginning to chip away at the cool barrier. I had started combing my hair a little differently, and had even broken into sitting with the "in" group in the lunchroom. Sure, not a big step for most people, but for me, a big change. I was working very hard to look like a cool graduating dude, and I had an opportunity to show it in front of the whole school.

I was one big step away from reaching the top, when my toe caught the edge of the last step. I fell forward, at full speed, sliding up onto the stage as if I were one of the trained seals performing for fish at Sea World. For a long second or two, there was absolute silence in the auditorium. Then, the crushing sound of every single person in the audience laughing hysterically, at me. So much for my big moment.

If I had ever had a chance to break out of the nerd category, it was gone now. My reputation was sealed. I had built that reputation over a young lifetime of being a good student, going to Church, becoming an Eagle Scout, not making any sports teams, not being elected to any school office or group, and now, being a total spaz.

If they had voted for the student who was "least likely to be a model", I would have been a shoe-in.

Taking The Country Out Of The Boy

My last semester of college, I scheduled interviews with recruiters from several companies who were hiring into their management training programs from our business school. After seeing a few of them, and not really feeling any good matches, I met with the recruiter from Southwestern Bell.

"Hello, I'm Happy Feller", he said. That was his real name, Happy. Most people might have made a comment or joked about it. I had a big advantage, having watched him play at the University of Texas. I had sold programs at college football games while in high school, and knew all about his days as UT's place kicker. I also knew that his father was the legendary Bob Feller, a major league baseball pitcher.

I got the job.

I went to work immediately, and set out to work my way up the corporate ladder. I worked in a local business office for a while, until I was chosen for a prestigious assignment, loaned to corporate headquarters in New Jersey. I flew in an airplane for the first time.

The most memorable parts of that assignment were the weekly trips a group of us took into New York City. Compared to the distances we drive to get places in Texas, driving through the tunnel from New Jersey into Manhattan was like driving to the mall. We did all of the regular tourist things, and then ventured farther and farther off of the beaten track. On a typical weekday evening, we would buy Broadway show tickets at the half-price booth, then go to dinner before the show. I saw a lot of the city, and learned my way around. This would become very helpful in the near future.

New York offered quite a few life lessons. Most of the people with me on that assignment had never met a person quite as naïve and inexperienced as I was at that time. When I first asked some of them to go to lunch with me, "I'm fixin' to go to lunch, you want to go with me?" brought an immediate "Fixin? Fixin? What's wrong with it? What are you going to do to fix it?" From that time on, the other guys always had a toothpick for me, and I played along, walking the corporate halls with a toothpick in my mouth. My nickname was "Texas" for the rest of the time there.

Keep in mind that I had grown up in small towns in Texas, with Dad leading the singing and Mom playing the piano at the local Southern Baptist Church. Mom sewed most of my clothes when I was a kid, and she cooked all of our meals. Nothing fancy, but good, simple meals. I had caught, skinned, and cooked my own catfish, but it never occurred to me what an uncooked shrimp looked like. The only kind of shrimp I had ever eaten was fried.

When a group of us went to a restaurant in the theater district, there was a big peel-and-eat-shrimp buffet. I went with all of the other guys, and loaded up my plate. When we sat down, I started popping them into my mouth, without looking around at anyone else to see how they were doing it. "This is terrible", I thought to myself, my mouth full of crunchy, tasteless stuff.

Just then, I looked around and noticed that everyone else had peeled the shell off the outside of the shrimp. I would have spit out the mouthful, but it was too late. Shrimp tastes much better without the shells. My learning curve was going to be very steep.

My instruction in fine dining came in some of New York's finest eating establishments, including Tavern On The Green. Lobster, crab, and other tricky eating assignments were completed with passing grades. The one thing that kept me out of trouble the most was that my mother had taught me well when it came to table manners. At least I knew which fork was for salads, and to keep my other hand in my lap. Thanks, Mom.

Model Employee

Back in Dallas, now on a staff assignment upgrading computer stations in all Dallas phone company business offices, I heard through the grapevine that Frank, one of my fellow management trainees, was a part-time model. He seemed to be able to handle his office job, while still being able to be a model. At first, I didn't really think much of it, but I stored it away for future use. I was challenged by the big project I had been placed in charge of, and had no time to think of anything else.

That was right before the big split-up of the phone company. All of a sudden, I was in the position of being the last guy on the list to get promoted, with dozens of candidates in front of me. I started doing the math. There were about twenty management employees at my level on the candidate list, with only about seven positions at the next level up, and they were all occupied. So many people had to get promoted, retire, or die before I would ever get a shot at the next level of management, that I started seriously thinking about other things to do for a living.

"Frank, I hear you model some." I managed to ask one day when we were in the same office, working on a project together. "How do I get started doing that? Do you think I can make any money at it?" I had dozens of questions for him, and Frank was patient enough to answer them all. "Well, the first thing you need to do is to get an agent. I'll give you some names of people to call, and you can go talk to them." He gave me the names of people at Kim Dawson, Sarah Norton, Tanya Blair, and Mike Beaty, which were the main agencies getting models work at that time.

I met with them all, and felt most comfortable with Mike Beaty, who ran his own small agency. He was a good old boy from Abilene, who had spent some time in New York, and seemed to know everybody in the business. I signed up with Beaty, primarily because there were far fewer guys who looked like me at his agency than at the other agencies. I bought into Mike's advice, "better to be a big

5

fish in a little pond, than a little fish in a big pond". At first, I felt more like a little fish in a little pond. I had several sessions of photographs taken, built a portfolio to show clients, and set out to be in business for myself as a model.

Moonlighting Model

For the first few months, I was still working my "day job", while trying to get away at lunch and personal time to go on interviews and jobs. It was very hard, but it was like starting a side business, and was easy to keep motivated to work both. There were a few awkward times, when someone would bring in a Walmart ad or some other little job I was in, and I had to face my coworkers.

"I've got a billboard job for you" the booking agent said, when I called in to check on things. "It's for a house builder, and you and a girl will be in a pool." "All right!" I said. This was the kind of job that didn't pay any more than a regular ad, but everybody in town would see it. It was a good job to get under my belt.

A couple of days before the job, a good friend of mine, a Dallas policeman, was killed in the line of duty. His funeral was the same day as the photo shoot. I paid my respects at the funeral, saw a few of my friends and talked about Ron, and then left to go do the modeling job. I felt a little guilty about leaving to go frolick in a pool with a girl for money, but I think Ron would have approved.

First big job on billboards & newspaper

The job turned out to not only be a billboard ad, but also ran in the newspaper. There were probably a thousand people that I came into contact with at my job, and it seemed that all of them had seen the ad. It was becoming harder and harder to avoid having people bring up that they had seen me in an ad.

Cattle Call

A lot of the work available for models at the time was through catalog houses, where newspaper inserts, direct mail catalogs, and other advertising for department and discount stores were produced. One of the biggest at the time, Mediagraphics, held monthly "go-sees", where all the models in town would stand in line for an audience with the head of the photography department, Tom. The word on the street was that Tom was pretty harsh, and that it was very hard to break into the rotation of working models at Mediagraphics.

One of the things most surprising to new models is just how many other models there are in town. All of the agents in town tell all of their models about each and every audition and go-see, and everybody who calls themselves models show up. If you didn't know what was happening, you might think the line was for concert tickets. Lines often snaked outside and around the buildings of the clients.

Standing in line with about two hundred other models, I wondered what kind of reaction I would have. Behind me and in front of me in line, I recognized a lot of faces from ads. Many models were asking to look at other models' portfolios, always exclaiming, "you've got a nice book", but really looking for an advantage or for ideas for the next photo shoot for their own portfolio. "I haven't got a chance", I told myself, noticing all of the magazine covers and professional work in their portfolios.

An hour after I stepped into line, I was next, and close enough to overhear the conversation between Tom and the model in front of me. Tom flipped through the pages quickly, one by one, saying nothing, reached the end, and then flipped even more quickly from back to front. As he reached the front, he slapped the book closed and never looking up, said "You've never worked here before, have you." The guy in front of me responded, "No Sir".

"You never will, either. Next". Uh oh. I'm toast.

"Hi, I'm Mike Ramsey. Nice to meet you, Tom". No response. He flips through my book exactly the same way he did with the poor guy who was in front of me, front to back, and back to front. Maybe he had seen my uneasy expression as I sat down, or maybe he thought I had a better chance than the guy in front of me, but I didn't get the "you never will" hammer to the skull.

I kept waiting for Tom to tell me some reason why they would not be using me, as he handed me my portfolio. He paused as we both touched the book, and said "Let me see your hands." I extended my hands, palms down, and then palms up. He didn't say anything. I took that as a positive sign. "Next", Tom barked.

I had no way of knowing just how often this scene would repeat itself over the next few years.

Watch Out For The Scout

"I've got an important appointment for you here at the agency", my agent said over the phone. Jake, a scout representing a Japanese model agency had scheduled auditions at the agency. "If you get picked for a trip to Japan, you can make a lot of money", he gushed.

I scheduled a time, not really expecting anything, but doing all of the things that I thought I was supposed to do to really be in the business. Like any other go-see, it seemed like every model in the universe was waiting in line to see the scout. Models who had returned from stints in Japan told of working almost every day, and bringing home very respectable paychecks. I waited my turn in line, trying to remain optimistic.

Jake claimed to have been a model, and had a few photos to back up his claim. Most looked like they all came from the same photo shoot in Hawaii. He was at the agency, and my agent recommended him, and I knew people who had gone to the agency he said he was representing. I had to treat this interview as a way to make a move up.

To my surprise, Jake asked me, "Do you want to go to Japan?" When I said "sure", he told me to get my passport up to date and get ready to go. "Wow! I'm going to Japan", I said to myself. I was excited at the prospects of making such a leap, but overwhelmed with all that I had to do to make the move.

"All right", I told myself, ".this is the point at which I make the leap". So, I gave my notice at the phone company, and got ready to go to Japan. I started making preparations to go out of the country for a while. This was to be my first big move in modeling. I was now committed.

Weeks passed, and I never heard back from Jake, or the Japanese agency. When I had my local agent contact the Japanese agency, nobody there knew anything about me, and I was not on their list of models they were expecting. While there were two or three models from our agency going, I wasn't one of them. Now what? I'm not going to Japan. I also have no job.

My agent didn't really have anything to offer in the way of an explanation as to why I was jerked around like that. At least I didn't pay any money for this lesson, with the exception that I no longer had a job. I wasn't the first person fooled by Jake "the snake", and I'm sure I wasn't the last.

Since I was now a full time model, I decided that I would go for it. I called up a friend, Ron, from my days at the phone company, who still lived in New Jersey, and made plans to take a little trip to see as many modeling agencies in New York City as possible.

If I was going to do this, I decided to do it all the way.

Trying To Break Into
The Big Time

I asked my agent for the names of the new talent directors or men's division heads of all the top agencies and made appointments to see as many as possible while I would be in the city. After weeks of calling and sending composite cards, I had appointments with the top three agents in New York City.

My first appointment was with the Zoli agency. When I met with the new talent director, he scanned through my portfolio, stared at me for several minutes, and then told me "your eyes are too close together". What? I got the impression that he felt his job was to come up with some reason why that agency wouldn't represent me, and that the eye comment was the first thing that came to his mind. Looking at myself in the mirror a little more closely, maybe he was right. My eyes are a little close together. The day was not starting off well.

Time to visit the second agency, Ford. When I got there, the guy I had the appointment with, was not there. No, there was no one else who could see me. Bye, and thanks for coming.

The agents at the Wilhelmina Agency made me feel a lot more comfortable, and they had some of the top talent in the business at the time, especially men. I met with the men's department head and the main booking agent for men. They agreed to represent me the following summer, if I would get my portfolio together better. OK, I've got a target to shoot for.

So I set out to save money and take tons of photos. I took any job I could get to make money between modeling jobs. I dug sprinkler system ditches for a landscaper friend, I valet parked cars at a hotel, I worked as a night manager of a 24 hour fitness club. I even tried my hand at selling timeshares in Tahiti.

During the time I parked cars at the Anatole Hotel, I had several occasions to speak with Kim Dawson, who was the first modeling agent in Dallas, and who had helped start the careers of many famous models. "Mike, Ramsey, isn't it? If you ever think about changing agencies, we would love to have you with us", Kim commented, as I opened the door to help her enter the car. Wow, here I was, a guy working for tips, holding the car door open for the biggest agent in town, and she knew that I was a model with another agency. I always remembered that, and near the end of my modeling years, I moved over to the Kim Dawson agency. She was a class act, and her agency is still considered to be one of the best in the world. I sometimes wish I had moved to that agency a lot earlier. But that might have spoiled a lot of the story.

Hercules Can Be Beaten

Right before going to NY, I went on an audition for a big job that all of the guys in town went on. It was a 7-Eleven ad for the 1984 Olympics, which would appear in every magazine in the country, promoting their sponsorship of the upcoming Olympic Games in Los Angeles. The decision on who to use for the ad came down to a choice between Kevin Sorbo's hand and my hand. We went to several auditions with the photographer, Charlie Freeman, as well as the advertising staff for Southland Corporation (the parent company of 7-Eleven), trying on the glove, holding the medals, and having polaroids taken. They liked something about my hand better and I was selected for the job.

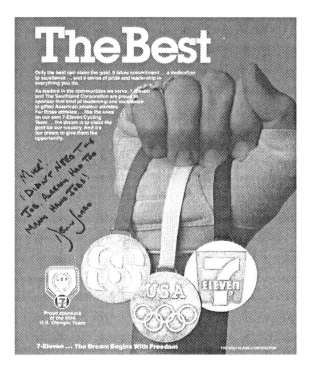

7-Eleven ad for '84 Olympics

The first time I met Kevin, he was the doorman at a club named "Confetti". Lots of models had jobs as greeters or doormen at nightclubs and restaurants, and it certainly helped to be a big, model-looking guy if you wanted to make a little extra money to keep you going in the model and acting business. Kevin was good for their business, both as someone who served as a good face at the door, as well as the occasional needed muscle when things went a little astray inside.

Kevin had been a college football player, and was very competitive. Not getting that job really bothered him. He was really mad about it, and was still visibly bothered by it more than a year later, when I ran into him again in Paris. When I contacted him recently, he was a terrific sport about it and even joked around about it. I think maybe time, and a string of movie and TV gigs, took most of the sting out of not getting that job.

Kevin Sorbo
as Hercules

I saw the ad in lots of magazines, but nobody knew it was my hand. Looking through the program at a Dallas Cowboys football game, my mother asked, "Isn't this your hand?" There it was, full page, right side, in living color. It was my first big hand modeling job, and I started adding "excellent hands" to my stats. I had no way of knowing that I was going to have to get used to people noticing parts other than my face.

I was in a business that prized recognizable faces, and my most famous feature was my hand.

Adventures With Air Marshals

So, off to NYC. Another Dallas model, David, was going to New York at the same time, and we decided to travel together. Keep in mind that we were both from little towns in West Texas. Traveling with a gun is a fairly normal thing for people from Texas, and David had packed his unloaded pistol in a case, and placed it in the suitcase he checked as baggage. I'm not sure if guns still make it through in the checked bags these days, since all luggage is much more heavily scrutinized. In those days, however, it was common practice.

People's Express was a brand new, startup airline, that was the very cheapest way to fly almost anywhere. No frills, no food, not even peanuts, but cheap. People's was the cheapest way to fly from Texas to New York at the time. The only trouble was that they only flew out of Houston. The good news was that the price from Houston to New York was so low, it was worthwhile to fly Southwest Airlines from Dallas to Houston, and then switch to People's Express for the flight to Newark Airport. David checked his baggage on Southwest, since there was no extra charge for checked baggage on Southwest.

One of the bad things about People's, and super low cost fares, was that you paid for every little thing. When we got to Houston, David was informed that he would be charged for each bag checked. Being cheap models, we wanted to save every dollar we could. I carried everything I owned in a backpack, a small bag, and a duffel bag. I had no problem putting all three of my bags in the overhead bins or under the seat in front of me.

David grabbed the bag he had checked from Dallas to Houston, to carry on to the plane for the flight from Houston to Newark, without thinking about what was in it. I cruised through the x-ray machine and when I looked back to watch David coming through, we both simultaneously realized that security guards were surrounding him.

I could barely keep up with the marshals as they ushered David into a little room. They were in there for over an hour, and gave me no idea how long David would be in there, or if was even coming out at all.

We had arranged to stay with David's aunt when we arrived in Manhattan, and I had no place to stay if I went on to New York without him. So, I had to wait for the outcome.

Luckily, the gun was not loaded, was locked in a case, and he had no record. Being in Texas helped quite a bit, too. He was allowed to ship his gun home, and was released. I'm sure he's on a list now, though. Thankfully, there was still another flight to Newark that night on People's Express, and we made it.

Young Man, There's No Need To Feel Down

David's aunt's brownstone was one of those rent-controlled places that nobody in New York ever lets go, once they have it. She had lived there for years, and intended to live there until she died. She was so happy to have two new people to talk to, all we had to do was buy groceries for rent.

There was one stipulation. New York is an inconvenient place to carry on a romance. When her boyfriend would visit once every couple of weeks, David and I would have to find another place to stay for a night. Easier said than done. Try finding a hotel in Manhattan, on a limited budget.

After asking around, the most logical place to stay was the YMCA. A room with two beds was only about $20, with a bathroom down the hall. David and I walked in, and I caught the guy's attention at the counter. "We need a double room for the night". Not knowing if this was his usual demeanor, I didn't realize until later that the look on his face was one of familiar disapproval. I didn't put two and two together at the time, but this was the place that inspired the Village People's song "YMCA".

Young man, there's no need to feel down.
I said, young man, pick yourself off the ground.
I said, young man, 'cause you're in a new town
there's no need to be unhappy.

Young man, there's a place you can go.
I said, young man, when you're short on your dough.
You can stay there, and I'm sure you will find
Many ways to have a good time.

It's fun to stay at the y-m-c-a.
It's fun to stay at the y-m-c-a.

They have everything for you men to enjoy,
You can hang out with all the boys...

It's fun to stay at the y-m-c-a.
It's fun to stay at the y-m-c-a

You can get yourself cleaned, you can have a good meal,
You can do whatever you feel...

No wonder the guy at the counter looked at us so funny when David and I walked up and asked for a room. Ironically, it was not a bad place to stay.

The agency sent me to see every photographer, magazine, and client on their client list. I even went to the paperback romance novel company, to audition for the cover photos. Those were the ones that Fabio became famous for. You know the ones, where the buffed guy with the frilly shirt, opened to show his chest muscles, holds up the fair maiden to plant the swoon-inducing kiss on her lips. They photographed models in action, and then painted the scene for the book covers.

They weren't interested in my face, but they liked my hands.

I auditioned for soap operas. "Take a few minutes to read over this script, and then read it to me, as you would on camera", the casting agent said, as she handed me the script from a recent soap episode. I read it, pretty well, I thought. "Not bad," she said cautiously, "Try it again, and this time, a little more animated." We did this a few times, and then she said, "Do you do any hand modeling?"

The early 1980s were great for male models, with GQ and other big-exposure jobs available. Everybody knew that if you got a job with Bruce Weber as the photographer, or a handful of other very recognizable clients, you immediately were going to make it in the business. This was the era before the magazines started using movie stars, pro athletes, and other celebrities for their covers, and making the cover of a magazine was the Holy Grail of models.

Magazine editors knew this. That is why models either didn't get paid or only received half rate for the cover of the magazine. They called it "editorial rate". The arrangement was, since you would receive a lot of publicity for being on the cover, and could reasonably expect to get a lot of future work from being seen by so many people in the business, that you would willingly work for less money. And you know what? They were right. Models would not only work for half rate, but probably would have paid almost any amount of money to be on the cover. It was that important.

Harlem Nights

Many businesses have company softball leagues, and the modeling agencies were no exception. "You want to play softball tonight?" one of the guys asked. "Sure", I said. I played on softball teams back in Dallas, and this seemed like a great way to fit into the agency. "You can ride with us to the game", volunteered the head of the agency's men's division. I borrowed a glove and hopped in his VW Rabbit, looking forward to showing them that I could play.

In Dallas, softball was always slow-pitch, where the ball is lofted lazily up into the sky, and floats down toward the plate, begging to be swatted out to the fence. This game was fast-pitch. Fortunately, I had played baseball, and a little fast-pitch softball, so I wasn't completely out of my element. One of the things I remember most about the game was feeling just a little bit intimidated by all of the guys that I had seen in magazine ads and on covers. Here they were, just regular guys, playing softball.

My first time at bat, on the first pitch, I shifted my weight back and swung with all my might. I flied out to left. "Oh well." I thought to myself, "At least I didn't strike out or bloop some wimpy pop fly". I didn't embarrass myself at bat, and even made some decent catches and throws from the outfield. All in all, it was a pretty good showing, for the first time out. The sun was beginning to set as we finished up the game. Good timing, since there were no lights on these fields.

The ball fields were in Randalls Island Park, accessible from the city only by the Triborough Bridge. As everybody was leaving, a couple in cars, but most on bikes, I asked my original driver about the return trip. "Sorry, but we're going the other direction. See you tomorrow at the agency." Because I didn't want to stand there looking stupid, as all the other guys left into the dimming light, I decided that I would walk.

As you cross over the West side of the Triborough Bridge, it becomes 125th Street. OK, I was staying on the West side of Central Park, on 76th Street. That's only 49 blocks, right? Not too far to walk. I walk from 76th down to 34th and back everyday, walking to the agency, and then walk dozens more blocks seeing clients. Piece of cake.

Those of you who know New York City are already ahead of me. For the education of those of you who have never been North of Central Park, the streets above 110th are a part of a very interesting part of New York City, called Harlem. As the sunlight dimmed lower and lower, there I was, a clueless Texas boy, walking with my backpack through the streets of Harlem.

Walking down 1st Avenue at first, then gradually moving West as I walked South, I sensed that I wasn't welcome. The guys standing at the street corners, and in front of the local bars, looked like they really wanted to give me a personal message. I think the only thing that kept some of them from confronting me was that I looked so out of place, I must have made them wonder what I was up to. What was this white boy doing walking down these streets, in the dark?

I was down below 120th now, and had moved over to 2nd Avenue. The scenery and the company were about the same. I walked West a block and South a block, 118th and 2nd, then 117th and 3rd, then 116th and Lexington, and so on. Finally, I saw a familiar sight, at 5th Avenue and 110th. Central Park at last! I am very glad that I didn't start any later.

The next day, when I told the other guys how I got home, they all thought I was crazy. In hindsight, so do I.

Being from Texas, I have always instinctively acted when I see somebody being treated badly. That's just the Texas way. You act first, and worry about what could have happened, later. One day, walking North through the wholesale floral district, on 7th Avenue, I heard a commotion in front of me. A yellow cab was stopped in the middle of a block and a guy was standing next to the driver's window, apparently struggling with the driver.

As I got closer, I could see that the driver was holding a nightstick with both hands, one hand on each end. The guy at his window had the middle of the nightstick in his left hand, and was punching the driver in the face with his right hand. He punched and punched that poor guy. I have no idea what the problem was, and didn't care. All I saw was a guy doing something to hurt another guy, so I walked up and shoved him away with one arm, and then walked off. The tough guy slammed his fist on the hood of the car and ran off.

As I walked past the corner, with fifty or sixty people standing around looking, a cop was standing there. I looked at him, not able to believe that a policeman had seen what I had seen, and not done anything about it. Maybe that was the way they do it in New York, but not in Texas. I decided that there were some things that I liked about the big city, but I didn't like the way that people didn't want to get involved.

Getting To Know My Gauche From My Droite

In planning my next moves with Wilhelmina, it had become obvious that going to Paris was an essential step in getting the big jobs in New York and in the fashion industry. One day, the Glamour Agency in Paris held auditions at Wilhelmina, looking for models willing to go to Paris to model. I met with Jean Francois, one of two brothers who ran the agency.

This was a lot better than most auditions I had been to, with no long lines, and a one on one conversation with the agent. I got the impression that this was a fairly exclusive, low volume go-see. Jean Francois asked me a few questions, such as "When are you planning to go to Paris?" and "Can you pay for your own ticket?" The importance of the second question would become apparent only after I had been in Paris a while.

"I look forward to seeing you in Paris", Jean Francois said. He gave me a handwritten invitation with all of the information I needed to bring with me to be represented by their agency. I had a report date, the address of the agency, and a personal invitation.

One of the first things I did was to go to the bookstore and buy a couple of French phrase books and tapes, to practice my French. I was determined to do this right. I carried around a little cassette player and listened on my headphones as I walked around town.

The cheapest deal I could find was a charter out of JFK on an old Boeing 707. That was a long flight on that little flying cigar. Cigar is an accurate description two ways, with the narrowness of the cabin, and since this was before non-smoking flights. I left NY one evening, and got there right at lunchtime in Paris.

Lunch in Paris is different than in the U.S. Everybody takes about two hours, beginning around 1:30 or 2:00. I lugged all my luggage up to the agency lobby, which was on the 1st Floor, which was actually the second floor. This took a little getting used to. The street level floor was called the Ground Floor, and what we call the second story was called the "premier etage", or "first floor".

Patrick (pronounced Patrique), Jean Francois' brother, who ran the men's department, came in and met with me. Patrick looked through my book, front to back, and back to front, just like dozens of people in the business have done before. I began to get a little nervous as he began mentioning other agencies that he would recommend that I go see. "I think you have a good look, but not quite right for us. I think you should see these agencies first", he said as he handed me a list of other Paris agencies. I was getting the big blow off.

Confused, I produced Jean Francois' letter inviting me to their agency. Patrick turned red as a beet when he read the note from Jean Francois. "Why did you not show this to me before?", Patrick asked. I had just assumed that Jean Francois had made the arrangements, and that everyone at the agency would know that I was coming. Another naïve assumption, based upon the Texas way. I need to stop doing that.

He had to take me now, but didn't like it one bit. Looking back on it now, I was finished before I ever started with Patrick, because he had already decided that I wasn't his kind of model, and only accepted me to honor his brother's invitation. The stage was set for me to be caught in the middle of their little family feud. I was doomed.

Mike's card, sent to Paris clients

I went out to see all of the clients and go on all of the auditions, but I wasn't going to be pushed by the agency. One of the other guys at the agency overheard me complaining that I was not getting work, and said, "I had the same problem when I first got here. I spent all of my own money, and was considering going home, when Jean Francois offered to loan me money. Now, the agency pays for my apartment, fronts me the money for all of my photos and composites, and even pays me money each week for food."

He went on to say, "When my bill got to around the $1000 mark, boom! All of a sudden, I started getting little jobs here and there. I've been working steadily since." Aha! They were making sure that they got their money back by recommending the models who owed the agency money, over guys like me who presented no risk of loss.

I had stumbled across a very important part of the game. The guys who were getting jobs were the ones who had not paid their own expenses, and were borrowing money from the agency. So, I started running a tab. When it reached $1000, surprise, surprise, I got a job.

Naked Ambition

There are two funny stories surrounding this first Paris job, the way I was chosen, and then the job itself. Originally, I was sent on an audition for some cologne or something, for which every male model in the universe was in Paris to audition for. I walked to the studio, turned the corner, and bam! A line of about two hundred guys, all with portfolios that included magazine covers, came out of the building and lined the street for about three or four blocks. It looked like the live version of GQ, all lined up in a row. So I stand at the back, feeling about as confident as Vanilla Ice at the Essence awards, and take my turn.

When my turn came, I found that the audition was to put on a little bikini underwear and stand facing a wall, with your hands up high, pushing against the wall. I overheard their comments in French about me (the phrase books and tapes were very helpful here), that I had girl hips. Fantastic, even the gay guys are cutting me down. Well, I didn't get that job, but that was the place that booked me for the hand work.

The actual job was with Claudia Church, who I knew from Dallas. I actually liked her and would have liked to have asked her out, but didn't have the nerve. I thought that maybe this was going to be the way to break the ice with her. Well, when we got on the set and found out what the job was, the ice was certainly broken!

The photographer gave me my instructions in English, but in a heavy French accent, "I want you to be on your knees behind Claudia. You will rub the lotion on her back, as if you were giving her a massage. Hold your hands like this." The French have a different way of doing many things, and why I was giving Claudia a massage while she was naked on all fours, I never understood. I often felt that they were just seeing what they could get away with, or what they could get us to do. Needless to say, there wasn't much talking going on during the photo shoot, between Claudia and myself. She was facing the wrong direction. When the job was finished, I didn't have the guts to ask her out or even ask for her phone number.

I received a pleasant surprise recently, when Claudia e-mailed me, thanking me for "not using the Paris photo" on a website where I had posted some photos from my modeling years. I used this one, where we were shooting some test photos.

Claudia & Mike on a test shoot

Claudia moved to Nashville and set out on a country music career. I even saw her on CMT (Country Music Television) one time, in the video for her hit song from her first album.

Claudia's 1999 CD cover

Budget Entertainment

Paris has a different schedule than we do in America. Lunch is a couple of hours in the early afternoon, and then everybody eats dinner at about 10:00 at night. After that, most cosmopolitan Parisiens go to their local nightclub for a little dancing and drinks. Models are always invited to make the places look better.

I wasn't really a nightclub person, but I was usually bored out of my mind, and was looking for something to do, especially if there were English-speaking people there. That usually meant American models. Models from our agency (and most other agencies) were granted free admission, so that was usually the entertainment most evenings.

The deal with models was, you got in free, but you had to pay for any food or drinks. This applied to the guys, but not the girls. Female models got a free ride, including their own bottle of booze. They had a bottle of their choice of alcohol, with their name written on it, and when they sat at a table, it was brought to them. Well, it didn't take long for the guys to figure out where to sit.

I could sit and drink all of the mixers that I wanted, such as Coke, orange juice, and tonic water, as long as the girls were at the table. The models were usually dancing with locals (that was the whole point of letting models in for free), so I usually sat at the table. It was a mutually beneficial arrangement, where I watched their purses and stuff, and I got free entertainment. It was better than sitting in an empty apartment.

One of the places we visited most often was Le Palace, a nightclub that had been built as a music hall in the 1920s. It was frequented by a lot of fashionistas, including many famous designers. One of my most vivid memories of Le Palace was the most regular of the visitors to the nightclub, Jean Paul Gaultier. He was there every single time I was there, and had a big, white bird on his shoulder, a cockatoo I think, each time I saw him. He had just hit it big with his first men's collection, and I don't know if he was really as weird as he looked, or was just putting on a show to build his reputation.

I'm Going To Rearrange
Your Face

Very few of the male models I met could be considered wimps, and quite a few of them were a little cocky and fight prone. These guys were pretty predictable, and you knew that they were telling the truth when they talked about getting into fights.

On the other hand, there were quite a few guys I met during the years, who claimed to have been involved in fights, usually telling of how they were jumped by groups of guys, and getting beaten up so badly that they required facial surgery.

Were they really jumped by gangs, or did they use these stories to explain away their cosmetic surgery? Well, in all of these cases, nobody witnessed the attacks. All of them were unhappy with their nose or other facial features. For some reason, admitting that you had a nose job made your appearance less "valid" or something, and people seemed to want to hide it. I really think these guys made up stories to establish plausible reasons for their change in appearance.

The women weren't immune to this, either. I know of quite a few "car wrecks" that precipitated new faces. I always found it odd that women would brag about a boob job, but would try to hide a nose job.

There seems to be some kind of taboo against admitting to cosmetic surgery in the business, even though everybody seems to have either had some or is planning to. For such pretty people, models sure are insecure about their attractiveness.

One of the oddest moments in my modeling years happened in Paris. Paul, John, and myself were roommates in a tiny Paris apartment, supplied by the agency. This typical model apartment had one bedroom, and I use that phrase generously, and a living room/kitchenette area, similar to a small efficiency apartment here in the U.S.

The bathroom was adequate, except for the fact that Paul spent an inordinate amount of time in there. John and I continually gave Paul a hard time about the amount of time he spent in there. He never had a good explanation about what was going on that took so much time.

Paul was from San Francisco, and seemed to be even more concerned with his appearance than the average model. He also seemed to be extremely self-conscious about the way his ears stood out from his head.

Sunday mornings in Paris may sound exciting, but one Sunday morning in the apartment, the three of us were eating breakfast while playing cards. John and I were facing each other, with Paul sitting in the middle of our semi-circle.

John and I both saw it in our peripheral vision at the same time. An odd movement caused us to both look up at each other, and we simultaneously realized what had just happened. That little flicker of movement, we now understood, was Paul's ear flicking out away from his head.

Now unable to hide his intricate work in the bathroom, he had to confess that he had been sticking his ears to his head, to avoid having them stick out so far in photographs. He showed us the little scars behind his ears, where the skin had been damaged by what he had used to stick his ears down.

He had been using SuperGlue, and holding his ears against his head with his hands, waiting for the glue to dry. That was why he needed to be in the bathroom for such long periods of time.

That incident, while hilariously funny at the time, made me really take a good look at the industry and what it can do to some people. The ability to put up with scabs behind your ears, caused by glue on your skin, makes even some cosmetic surgeries look sane.

You Don't Have To Go Home,
But You Can't Stay Here

Some of the younger guys, who had chosen to let the agency pay for their tickets to Paris, were beginning to get homesick and wanted to go home. This is where the importance of paying your own way comes in.

In exchange for paying for their round-trip airfare, the models had agreed to let the agency hold their passport as security. Big mistake. Many an unsuspecting model was taken advantage of by unscrupulous agents, holding that trump card.

One of the most telling episodes of how the agents in Paris treated models was with the example of a young, high school girl from Canada, who had won a modeling contest. Her prize for winning was a contract with the Paris agency, room and board for the summer, and a magazine cover photo shoot.

Near the end of her stay, right before going back to school, she still had not received the magazine cover session she had been promised. Able to speak French fluently, she berated them into agreeing to do it. The client came to the agency to meet with her, and everything was arranged. She would get her magazine cover.

At the end of the meeting, the magazine owner said to the model (all of this conversation in French), "Are you coming with me?" She did not understand. The magazine owner repeated, "Time for you to go home with me." The model then understood exactly what was going on. She began screaming at the man, who had made it clear that she was expected to go home with him, in exchange for being on the cover of his magazine.

Shockingly, the agents began yelling at the model, angry that she had embarassed them in front of their client. They were made at HER. Evidently, he usually got what he wanted. Not this time. The model quickly was sent back to Canada, but not without her magazine cover she was promised.

I decided that Paris was not for me, or maybe Paris decided that I wasn't for it. Fortunately, I had my own ticket home.

Back In Dallas

New York and Paris were useful to me when I came back to Dallas. Clients were impressed when my local agent told them I had just arrived from Europe. The photos from Paris were very good, and made my portfolio look a lot more professional. I started getting some big jobs in Dallas. I was cast for the Aramis international TV commercial, seen everywhere in the world, except the United States. I was the first Reed St. James guy, featured in Haggar's ads (shown below) for their attempt at upscale men's clothing.

Reed St. James ads

I started working regularly for all of the local department stores. All of this was full body stuff, but didn't make me a household face. I had a great portfolio, with a lot of actual jobs in it, but I was still very much an unknown.

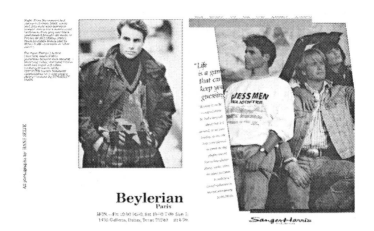

Dallas department store ads

I'll bring up more later about how important it is to have an agent, but the first Reed St. James job was a great example of how having a good agent can make all the difference in the world when it comes to getting paid.

I was booked for the very first Reed St. James ad, the same day that I found out my agent was closing its doors. I struggled with thoughts of whether I would get paid for the job, as I stood on the set and posed for the shots. I was really worried that I was working for free that day.

First Reed St. James ad

I signed their release, and then wondered what to do with the invoice. I thought about just submitting the invoice directly to the advertising agency, but it likely would have taken a while to get paid, and would make it obvious that I didn't have an agent.

I quickly signed with another agent, and did get paid for the session fee. I was paid $250 for the ad. For that moment, I was happy to get paid.

I forgot about the job, partly because I was beginning to get more and more work, but also because the Reed St. James people were booking me for more ads.

Remember the release I had signed? It released any rights I had to how the image was used. Normally this works just fine, since the ads are usually only for print ads, such as magazines. In some cases, when the client knows that they will use it for wider distribution, such as billboards, packaging, or TV, there is a higher negotiated rate.

Without an agent to negotiate at the time the job was booked, I had no negotiating power or knowledge of the client's intent. A few months later, I saw the ad as a sponsor at the end of Wheel of Fortune. What should have generated a fairly big bonus for TV use, turned out to net me absolutely nothing but the original session fee.

I learned a hard lesson there. <u>Always use an agent to book your jobs and bill your invoices.</u> <u>Not only do you get extra help in collecting the money you know you are owed, you also have someone who knows the right questions to ask.</u>

This Time I'm Really Going To Japan

"Captain", as he was called by everybody in the business, was the scout for the Daisho agency, in Osaka Japan. I met with him at my Dallas agency, and I was invited to come to Osaka. This time it was for real.

I had the option of buying my own tickets, or having them provide them and then taking the money out of my salary from jobs in Japan. After doing some calculations with the yen-to-dollar exchange rate, I decided that I would take my chances on paying my own way. I was able to find a cheaper flight than the one they would have paid for, anyway.

Japan is very strict with its immigration laws, and there are very specific visas that are available. You have to choose either a 60 day visa, which can be renewed indefinitely by leaving the country and returning with the renewal, or a one-time 90 day visa, which requires at least a year between visas. Most models choose the 60 day visa, and leave for a week or two to get the visa renewed. Many models I met while in Japan, had lived there for many years, leaving for a vacation to Okinawa or Hong Kong every 60 days. I met one guy who claimed to have been able to save a million dollars over a ten year period. I didn't make that much.

I did a ton of work there, including some big stuff for Toyota and Asics. Even in Japan, I was recognized as having the kinds of hands they needed to look "American". One of my first big jobs was for a magazine ad, where my hand was painted up to look like a snake, and was placed on the female model's leg.

Japan ad for department store

Japan was different in many ways, many of them fundamental. One example was on my first job there. On the set, the photographer began signalling me with his hand. The gesture was with his palm facing the ground, waving his fingers in the way I would use to signal, "move back". He was saying "skoshi" (just a little, in Japanese) as he motioned this way. So, I moved back a little.

"Iye, iye. Skoshi", ("No, No. A little closer."), and he began using both arms to indicate to come closer to him. The sign I interpreted as meaning to scoot back, was actually a sign to come closer. Up is down and down is up. I had a lot to learn about Japan.

I did learn a lot, and worked a lot. I did regular clothing jobs for department stores and similar clients, but I kept getting jobs that showed my hands, with clients such as Panasonic. I would push a button, or hold a device, and look American.

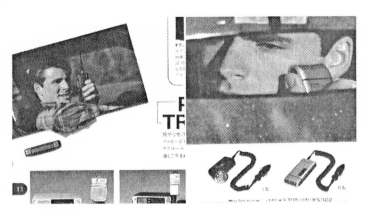

Japan clients like Mike's hands, too

The timing of me being in Japan could have been a little better. Not long after I arrived, the month of August, 1985, the fortieth anniversary of a very important world event occurred. The usually courteous and mild mannered Japanese people were inundated with images of what had happened in Hiroshima and Nagasaki forty years earlier. And there I stood in their midst, on the trains and in the street, representing the people who brought that misery to them. It didn't help that I was almost a foot taller than everybody.

Fortunately, that uncomfortable situation faded over the next few weeks, and I was treated with the usual friendliness of the Japanese people.

Japan has a sort of paranoia about foreigners, some of it warranted, some not. There were legitimate reasons why they so mistrusted models. One of the guys I worked with in Osaka, a guy from Italy, was jailed not long after I arrived for selling marijuana. My first taste of this scrutiny was when my mother sent me a box of chocolate chip cookies for my birthday. When I opened the box, it was just a bunch of crumbs. There was not one cookie that had not been completely smashed, in the attempt to search for potential drugs. That's just the way they do it over there. I came to expect that all packages would be opened before I saw them, and they were.

Just like the clubs in Paris, the nightclubs in Japan had deals with the modeling agencies, to allow us to get in free. They also knew it was good for business to have gaijins (foreigners) in the nightclubs, especially if they were models. Models were just below rock musicians and actors on the celebrity scale there, and we were a draw for their business.

One of the oddest things I noticed about the Japanese dance clubs was the fact that almost every one of them had a big wall on at least one side of the dance floor, completely mirrored. What made this mirror wall even more odd was that the locals would line up, face the mirrors, and watch themselves dance. The only times they weren't watching their own moves, was when they were watching ours. Back in the U.S., I never was really known as a great dancer, but you would have thought that I was Michael Jackson to these guys. They copied every step I danced, and then worked the mirror to make sure they were doing it correctly. I got a kick out of it every time.

I profited handsomely from Japan, both financially and in experience. Most importantly, I was ready to come back to the U.S. and make some money in modeling.

Sampling of Japan ads

Transition Into Parts Modeling

Not long after I got back from Japan, I was chosen to be the first Fossil guy. At the time, the company was two brothers, one who was a buyer at a local department store, and the other who took designs to Hong Kong for production. As you might know, the company went on to become a huge player in the fashion watch business, and has since gone public and added fashion lines, and even opened some retail stores.

Fossil Watch ads

I did a lot of work for Fossil, and since they made watches, my hands were a big reason, and were featured in most of the ads. They needed a guy with a face and good hands, so at least I got some exposure. It was also a lot of fun to have met and worked with people who went on to great business success.

I started getting a lot of work from Radio Shack at this point. I held a lot of cellular phones, typed on a lot of PC keyboards, and pointed at a lot of calculators and other electronic devices. This was the beginning of the serious hand modeling work. I began to make as much money, and maybe even more, from hand modeling than from all other types of modeling work.

Radio Shack ads & magazine covers

Travel Years

During 1986 and 1987, I travelled all over North America. I went to Atlanta, Chicago, LA, and even Mexico. One of the biggest jobs I had was on a L'Oreal shampoo commercial shot in Mexico City. Renee Simonsen was under contract with them at the time, and she was being featured in the commercial. My role was to come in and kiss her on the cheek, in the "after" shot. Of course, like with most commercials, take after take was required, and I had to kiss her on the cheek over and over and over again. Tough job, but someone has to do it.

This was a worldwide commercial, shown everywhere except the U.S. I found out later, the reason why these commercials were not being shown in the U.S., was because they didn't want to have to pay the royalties in the U.S. market, and could simply "buy out" the talent fees.

I made a lot of money during this period, but spent a lot of money on airfare, hotels, and rental cars. I worked with quite a few big clients such as Black&Decker, Color Tile, Coor's Light, Land's End, Sears, and Montgomery Wards. But, the trend continued. Most were either hands only, or because they needed good hands to go with a face.

It became almost bizarre. One job I did for Black & Decker in Chicago, I flew from Dallas to Chicago, rode the A Train in from the airport, came out of the train station, walked one block to the studio, shot the photo all day, and then went back to the train, to the airport, and flew back to Dallas. All of this for a hand shot. In the ad on the right, I'm the guy on the right, holding the sander. I guess a good hand is hard to find.

Land's End and Black & Decker ads

I started getting more TV commercials during this period, and the money got better. In one instance, I did a brief appearance in a Color Tile commercial that played only three days, which paid me over $4000.00.

Some of the jobs I found funniest were similar to the Coors Light TV commercial I did. It was similar to the current ones, where girls in skimpy outfits and buffed guys are all having a wonderful time out barbecueing and playing volleyball. Then my part was, sitting in a cylinder of white foam core walls, pulling the tab on can after can of beer. It was slippery, because they spray the cans with glycerine to make the beads of "condensation" look prettier. And, I couldn't see what I was doing, since my head couldn't be in the reflection of the silver can. I had to sit outside the box, sticking my arms and hands in, while I tried to move where they wanted me to by their voice commands.

What most people don't know, even those in the modeling business who haven't done parts modeling, is just how long it takes and how involved it is to shoot a hand or parts shot. The shots of the frolicking models may have taken a few hours, but then setting up my shot, shooting it and breaking it down afterward, took even longer. Everybody stood around watching me stick my arm into a white box, with the director saying, "rotate 5 degrees clockwise", or "move away from camera a quarter inch".

That's pretty much the way most hand jobs went. If I could have detached my arms, and still made them move robotically, I would have been much more comfortable. You wouldn't believe the contortions that I sat through. It's a job.

Money Years

From 1988 through 1991, when I "retired" from modeling, I made a good living in "show business". I not only did fashion and commercial print modeling, but also did TV commercials, industrial films, all kinds of parts jobs, and even did voice over work. I was one of the top, if not the top male model in Dallas.

This was about the time that JCPenney came to town, and started using Dallas models for their ads and catalogs. There was a lot of work to spread around among the local models, and I got my share of it.

JCPenney ads

Even though I was working regularly in ads that showed my face, I was still working even more in jobs that either did not show my face, or that cast me in unusual situations.

My first big magazine cover was for Texas Monthly, where I was to portray a hospital patient, illustrating the cover story. Unfortunately, this potential career booster followed my pattern of obscuring my face with an oxygen mask.

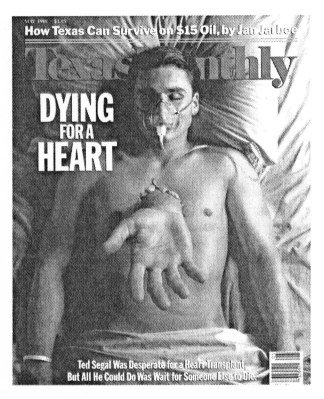

Mike's first big cover, but face covered

While the cover got a lot of attention, and it helped the photographer's reputation and business, nobody could tell it was me.

One day, standing in the checkout line at the grocery store, I was able to overhear the conversation in front of me. "Ewwww, that's so gross", said one lady to the other. They stood in line and looked at the cover for a while, and then, each of them bought one.

Meanwhile, right behind them, was the guy in the photo, but they didn't recognize me. I know quite a few models who would have made a point to let the women know that they were the person on the cover, but I actually got a kick out of the situation.

I was used to not being recognized and already had begun to appreciate the irony. The good news was that the photographers appreciated the way I worked with them, and these publicy unrecognized photos were beginning to get me even more jobs that paid well, but left me essentially anonymous.

Runway Modeling

The first runway show I ever did was as a replacement for a guy named Marty, who had to bow out at the last minute. This show was a dance-oriented show, as part of a hair show. Most of the models were showing off the handiwork of local hair salons, but there was also a regular runway show, displaying fashion clothing. The part that Marty had been cast for was as one of the fashion runway models, doing the "moon dance". Marty could do it well, but I could only do it in my socks. Marty told them I was very good at it.

This was my first runway job, so I didn't want to blow it. I knew that if I didn't do a good job, not only would I not get any more of these types of jobs, but that I would let Marty down, since he had recommended me.

I was dressed up like a police officer, and my only job was to come out and moon dance at a particular part of a song. I managed to look like I knew what I was doing enough to get through rehearsals. While we were getting ready for the show, one of the main male dancers, who evidently had taken a fancy to me, kept hanging around me and squealing, "Frisk me! Frisk me!"

This was my first runway show, and the first time I was hit on by a guy.

Most of the runway shows I worked, women were the main feature and men were accessories, props, or an afterthought. Because of this, most runway shows, even the ones that feature men's clothing, have far greater numbers of women than men in the cast. This makes the backstage area quite interesting for the lucky few guys who like women.

In print modeling, about one half of the male models were gay. In runway modeling, the percentages of gay to straight men are much different. Because runway walking requires a little more style and smoothness, models need to be able to be a little more extroverted. Usually, the gay guys were better at that. I didn't have that naturally, but since it was a job, I learned how to look like I did.

You do a lot of standing around in your underwear backstage of runway shows. There are racks of clothes to wear, and there is very little time to try them all on, get the buttons and ties ready to speedily pull them on for changes, so there is a lot of time spent changing clothes.

It was not a big deal for me to see guys in underwear, but seeing a lot of beautiful women, relaxing backstage in underwear, took a little getting used to.

Backstage Breast Chicken

There is a traditional "game" played by teenage boys in Texas, where one boy puts his hand flat on a table, palm down, while another stabs a knife between the outstretched fingers, as quickly as possible. Flinch by moving your hand away, and you lose. Stab the guy's finger, and of course, the guy with the knife loses. The game was called chicken.

Most of the female runway models had implants. One interesting phenomenon I have observed in women with implants is, they like to show them off. Since most of the guys were gay anyway, the girls felt comfortable walking around topless.

"Mike, I hear you're a triathlete", said a six feet tall, one hundred and fifteen pound, 34C model. "How do you do that?" she asked, less than one foot away from me. I am certain that she was trying to get me to look down, since she and all of the other female models were completely topless. If I didn't appear to look, I must be gay, but if I looked, she would win the game of "breast chicken". What she either didn't know or didn't care about was that peripheral vision allowed me to see just fine, while never looking away from her eyes.

I won.

This scene occurred several times over the years, backstage of runway shows. I came to the conclusion that it was a game with the women. It was clearly a game of chicken, to see if I would look down, or be able to keep my eyes on theirs. I don't know what they thought of me, but I never looked down.

Underwear Modeling

"OK, are we ready?", the photographer asked. "Are you feeling all right?", obviously noticing how pale the ten year old blonde boy appeared, standing next to me. "You don't really want to be here today, do you", I said, half a question, half an observation. I had noticed his mother pacing at the back of the studio, looking more like a tiger in a cage at the zoo, than an interested observer.

We were each wearing a white T shirt and white briefs, modeling for a Wal Mart ad. He shook his head no, and kept glancing toward his mother, as if he were performing more for her than for the photographer. He was pale and looked like he was going to be sick.

We spent the usual fifteen or twenty minutes standing there on the set, while the photographer and his assistant adjusted the lights and cameras. The boy's color drained to almost the color of the white underwear, and he had stiffened up his stance. Just as the photographer was ready to begin, I heard and felt what obviously was his breakfast of hurled Fruit Loops on my feet.

The good news was that I was barefoot, with no socks or shoes to clean up, and that I was on the clock for the time it took to find a replacement kid.

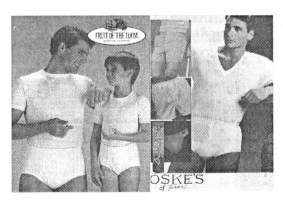

Underwear ads required tucking/smoothing

55

The best part about underwear jobs was that we got time and a half. Men didn't always get this premium rate for underwear shots, but the bigger clients usually paid it. Women had a much sweeter deal available for them. In addition to the time and a half rate available for bathing suits and other revealing clothing, there was also a double rate for all sheer underwear, such as lingere.

The most embarassing part of underwear jobs for me was not being on the set in my underwear, it was the things I had to do to prepare for the photo. If I didn't have a good pair with me, I would have to go to the grocery store or convenience store to buy a pair of women's pantyhose. I used this pair of pantyhose, with the legs cut off, to use as a liner under the briefs. This was necessary to make all of the "parts" appear smooth. The goal was to cover up the fact of what was actually there. This was accomplished with artful tucking and smoothing, and was successful if there was only the slightest indication of something less than a flat surface, but no distinguishable features.

Models get used to being in their underwear, having to wait around in dressing rooms or backstage of runway shows. They often have to get makeup done before the clothes go on, so they sit around in their underwear. After a while, it stops being something you are even aware of.

Like most of the guys, I would have done those jobs for regular rate, but the extra money was always nice.

Off With His Head

One of the most overlooked aspects of modeling is that of full body, without head showing. This might be shot from the waist down, for jeans, pants, or shoes, or could be a full length shot, with only the head cut off.

Jobs that paid well, but only neck down

The pay for such jobs is the same as for regular ad work, but you can't really use the tearsheets as marketing tools. It's also very difficult to prove that the rear end in the photo is actually yours. I don't know how many of these types of ads I have accumulated over the years.

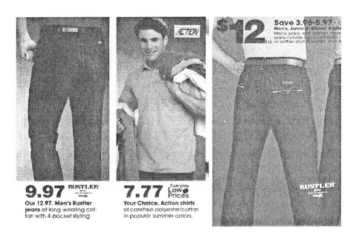

Jean ads look better than real life

Take a good look at the photo above, on the right. Those jeans look like they fit perfectly, right? The crease is nice and straight, and they look perfect. Only people in the business know that jeans just don't really look that way. To get them to look this way, you have to have clamp-on weights attached to the bottom of the jeans, just out of sight of the camera. These weights, pulling down on the fabric, make the jeans look nice and smooth, giving the appearance of perfect fit.

Often, even more drastic measures have to be taken to make clothes look like they fit. Clothes are often cut with scissors to make them loose in certain areas, pinned to make them look more tailored, and even taped together with duct tape. I wish I could have saved some of the polariods taken from the side away from the camera, showing the chaos of the backside of the clothes, in contrast to how perfect they appear in the ads.

Don't ever worry that clothes don't fit you the way they look on the models in the ads. They don't fit the models that way, either.

There is not really any way to pursue this type of modeling as your main focus. It is just extra work that your regular clients will throw your way occasionally, often while you are already there for another shot. It is a way to maximize the amount of ads shot, and minimize the number of models needed that day at the studio.

This is not an area of modeling that people who have great bodies, but less than perfect faces can break into. You can't just walk in and announce that you do pants modeling. You will be booked on this type of job, mainly because the client likes your overall look, and will most likely use you for regular photo shots, in addition to these jobs.

Any job is a good job. I advise models to take the money, even if you can't use the tearsheet. You never know when that client may like you and book you for the next job, showing your face.

My motto was that today's job is the best chance you will ever get to audition for tomorrow's job.

Assorted Parts

A sort of side business of the parts modeling jobs, are those which feature the head or feet or other parts, to sell clothing, devices, or whatever. Examples of this are sunglasses ads, ads for hats, and ads for footwear.

Assorted ads for head, hands, & feet

Just like the rear-view pants modeling jobs, these jobs are almost never cast with parts models, but usually feature regular models. They are often added on to the booking of a model who is there for a full-length photo session, as a way to get as many photos taken as possible, in as short of a time and for as little money as possible.

Fitness Modeling

A lot of models could get away with smoking, drinking, and partying, and still be able to keep their bodies looking good. My genetics did not allow me to do that. In fact, I had to work out like a madman to stay small enough to fit the sizes clients provided.

I liked a lot of sports, and played on basketball, flag football, and softball teams, and enjoyed running, biking, and swimming. As I got in better shape, I discovered that I enjoyed competing in triathlons. Training and racing in events that combined swimming, cycling, and running not only helped me to keep my body looking the way clients expected, but also gave me a gimmick. Since triathlons were still new at the time, it was something interesting for clients to talk to me about.

As more and more clients learned about the sports activities I was competent performing, they started steering me jobs that required simple athletic photo sessions. Ads for treadmills, stair steppers, weight machines, bicycles, and other sports, were available to me with some of the clients I used to only do clothing ads for.

Being known for parts modeling helped me to combine this reputation with the newly acquired athletic work, and I was able to promote myself as a model who could look good using a lot of equipment. Sunglasses, boating equipment, and nutrition products were ads that my clients found me uniquely qualified to appear in.

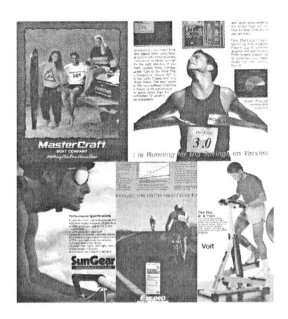

This was far before there was any fitness modeling category, and I know of no one at the time who called themselves a fitness model. While I was never actually called a fitness model, I was one of the early pioneers in that offshoot business.

Now, there are whole agencies dedicated exclusively to fitness models. They are very specialized, and it is very hard for one person to be in both fitness modeling ads and regular modeling ads. You don't see many models from Men's Fitness, for example, also in GQ.

This WCT poster was a limited edition

Resort Hotel Brochures

Some of the more fun jobs, even if they didn't pay quite as well, were the ones where I was booked to be in the brochures of resort hotels. Most of them were in Mexico, but I also did one for a hotel in Antigua (more on that one later). I even was chosen to visit Acapulco and Puerta Vallarta several times.

"We're looking for a model who is a certified scuba diver", said Warren, the advertising agency executive with a chain of Mexican hotels as his major client. I showed him my PADI scuba certification card, and I was in. I was to be one half of a pretend loving couple, vacationing in Cozumel.

These weeklong jobs usually paid only about the amount we would normally get for a full day of photography modeling, but it was pretty close to a paid vacation. Of course, all of the travel and lodging were paid for, but also all food and incidentals. We even had free use of the room mini bar, within reason.

Don't think that these jobs are no work and all play. While the work is pretty good when you can get it, there really is very little free time. Most of the day is spent taking photographs of every aspect of the hotel. Shots of the couple as they check in at the front counter. Drinks in the lobby bar. Then there was lounging at the pool, dinner in the restaurant, the breakfast buffet, local attractions and entertainment, guest rooms, and of course, the Presidential Suite. The job was to show everything that the hotel wants people to see about their property.

When we weren't actually shooting, we were changing clothes for the next scene, or waiting in our rooms for the light to be just right. I watched quite a few cable movies during these weeks, in thirty-minute increments. The only real free time was at dinner, where the whole crew ate together.

Typical hotel resort brochure job

The Cozumel job was one of the best of these resort jobs. As a diver, I really enjoyed the whole day spent on the diving shots. We rode a boat out to some wrecks, dove once in the morning, had a lunch of fish caught while we were diving, then an afternoon dive, and the trip back to the island on the boat.

After that long day, and then a nice dinner, I slept like a baby. If I could get that kind of work every day, I'd do nothing else.

Make Them Remember You

Photographers, stylists, and advertising agency employees are just like people in any job. It doesn't take very long before even the most exciting job becomes just a job. Even the most glamorous swimsuit issue photo shoot can become tedious.

I gradually figured out what some models knew instinctively, or lucked into. You have to have some kind of gimmick that makes clients remember you. Most importantly, it doesn't really matter why they remember you, just that they remember you.

One example of a model who always had clients talking about him, was a guy named Greg. Greg was a good-looking guy, I guess. He got his share of work in town. Everybody in town seemed to know him, and also seemed to like him.

I worked with him often, and while he was a nice enough guy, I didn't see anything spectacular about his personality or wit or intelligence, justifying his popularity. I finally found out on one trip to Puerto Vallarta for one of the hotel brochure jobs.

There were two couples on the trip. Greg was teamed with a woman, as was I, and we were working separate versions of the hotel's advertising. Greg and his "date" were in the print version, and my "other half" and I were in the video version. We basically did the same scenes, one couple in still photography, and then the same scenes recorded on video.

The job went along normally, but the crew kept hinting around about Greg's reputation as a goofy guy. It sounded like he was there for entertainment value. I didn't quite understand exactly what was up, but the crew certainly expected something from him, and soon.

We didn't have to wait long. That night, as I was walking down the hallway to my room, Greg stuck his head out of the door to his room. He was checking out the room service tray on the floor across the hall. There seemed to be a lot of uneaten food on the tray.

He was going to eat it.

I laughed and went on to my room, thinking to myself how funny the story would be the next day when we talked about Greg eating somebody else's room service leftovers.

As I closed the door behind me in my room, I heard Greg beating on his door. Wondering what was going on, I looked out in the hall, to see Greg moving quickly away from me, down the hallway, with only a potted plant behind him, and another in front of him.

When he had left his room to pick up the room service tray, his door had locked behind him, leaving him naked in the hallway.

Now I knew why all the clients knew Greg. They booked him for jobs, expecting exactly this kind of event, providing months and months of entertainment on the job.

Most models would prefer not to have that kind of reputation, just to have clients remember them and book them, but it seemed to work well for Greg. The rest of that week, Greg not only didn't seem to mind that everybody knew about what happened, but played right along, poking fun at himself. Greg was either really smart, and knew how to use self-deprecating situations to advance his career, or was really dumb and lucky.

As I eventually learned, it didn't really matter which one was the case. All that mattered was that people remembered Greg, and talked about him.

The closest I had to such a reputation was that I was a triathlete. At that time, it was still new enough of a sport to be considered eccentric.

Fortunately, there were a few photographers and other clients who were cyclists or triathletes themselves. Booking me for jobs allowed them to talk about their hobby on the set, and made their job more fun.

I didn't play this angle up nearly as much as a very well known model, Ed. Ed would take up almost any sport, as soon as he found out that a photographer he wanted to work with liked it.

He bought a ski boat and took out one photographer who was an avid skier. He bought a really nice racing bicycle and rode with a photographers who were competitive cyclists.

Ed did very well this way. I watched and learned, even though I didn't feel comfortable going to quite that extreme.

Don't Promise What You Can't Deliver

"Do you play tennis?", the ad executive asked. "We need models to play tennis at the P.V. (Puerta Vallarta) Newcomb's Tennis Ranch. You don't need to be a pro, but you have to look like you can really play".

I played quite a bit in college, and had already played tennis for the photos for several brochures for the same ad agency's Mexican hotel clients. "You bet", I replied.

The female model, which had been tentatively selected to go with me on the shoot, said "Yes, I can play tennis", confidently.

The first day on the job, dressed for tennis, the client announced, "We're going to start on the clay court". "I've never played on clay before", I said apologetically.

"Let's see what you can do", he said, and sent me out with the local pro to volley a few hits back and forth. "You're fine. Now let's see you out there, Debbie", he said to the female model.

After two or three attempts to hit the ball, it became shockingly clear that Debbie had never played tennis. "I thought you said you played tennis", scolded Warren. "I can, just not very well", offered Debbie.

Warren, barely containing his anger, announced he would look around for a visitor of the resort to play tennis with me. He found one, we played a few games for the camera, and we salvaged the shot.

This is an important point to make about being honest about skills. On auditions, I have heard actors and models say "yes", when asked if they could jump on a trampoline, ride a motorcycle, roller skate, swim, ride a bike, or any number of physically demanding activities.

I don't remember any of them ever saying "no", even though they knew full well that if they were actually required to perform these feats, they would have to admit that they were unable or unqualified to do them.

Not only is this dishonest, but there is a real danger of injury or even death in these situations. Models and actors are playing with fire when they claim expertise in things they have no experience with. I can only imagine what might happen if a non-diver were to go on the scuba job I had worked on, for example.

I have a clear conscience when it comes to the things that I said I could do for modeling and acting jobs. I always made sure that I never claimed to be able to perform any activity that I was not at least mediocre in ability with, and always informed the clients about my honest level of ability.

It may have cost me a few jobs, where another model or actor got away with a misrepresentation, but it only takes one situation where they are caught in a lie, to kill their future prospects.

Honesty is always the best policy.

Paradise Shloshed

"Your're a diver, right Mike?", asked Angela, the wife of a well known local photographer, who also worked as the stylist on many of his shoots. "That's great. We've got a trip coming up in a few weeks in Antigua, and we need a diver for some of the hotel shots."

I was booked for the job, along with a female counterpart, and we were off on one of these pleasant work/vacation trips.

I had worked with Angela quite a few times before, but I had never had a chance to work with Ren, her husband. I was looking forward to both the nice location, and working with a good photographer.

The resort was everything it was promised to be in the sales materials, and the weather was as a resort should be. It was promising to be one of the best resort jobs yet.

I had barely checked into my room, and was unpacking my suitcase, when Angela knocked on the door, asking "Mike, do you mind if we borrow a few bottles from your mini bar? We want to make sure that we don't run out of our favorites." "No problem", I said, since I didn't drink anyway. I didn't think much about it at the time.

And when Ren came by later and asked if I was drinking one particular brand of alcohol, and then also took those from my room, while it seemed odd, I was working for him, and I was not responsible for paying for what was used from the minibar, anyway.

Pretty soon, however, it started to become obvious that Ren and Angela were pounding down the little bottles of booze, pretty much non-stop.

"Phyllis, have either Angela or Ren come to your room to borrow the little bottles of booze?", I asked the woman with us on the shot. "Yes, I thought it was so weird. They have both been a couple of times. I don't have any left in my mini bar."

I started seeing the picture very clearly during the hotel lobby shot. The photographer's assistant, Jaime, had set up a ten-foot ladder, to allow the Ren to shoot the photo from above. As Ren was trying to focus the camera from atop the ladder, he just almost fell off.

At this point, Jaime volunteered to do the focusing, while Ren stood next to the ladder, on solid ground, holding the extension cord to open the shutter.

That's how the photos were taken. Jaime would do all of the work, focusing the camera and getting the shot ready, and Ren would go "click".

Normally, in photo sessions of a bar or using what appear to be alcoholic drinks, fake drinks are used, without alcohol. In this scene, Angela had specifically instructed that real drinks be made.

I didn't think much about it until after the shot was finished, when Angela and Ren sat down and polished off the "prop" drinks.

The entertainment got even better that evening after dinner. I was enjoying a little private time, sitting in a chaise lounge on the beach, relaxing in the moonlight, when Angela came up to me and asked, "Have you seen Ren?" "No, I haven't. If I do, I'll tell him you're looking for him, though."

A few minutes later, Phyllis snuck up and sat down in the chair next to me, and sounding a little out of breath, said "Ren's been chasing me all over the place. He's drunk and trying to hit on me. What do I do?"

"I'll walk you to the room. Just stay there, and he'll have forgotten all about it in the morning. Just pretend it didn't happen", I said, half trying to convince her, and half myself.

Sure enough, he never remembered a thing. Angela did, though. It didn't seem to bother her enough to stop visiting our rooms for the little bottles of booze, though.

I can't find any copies of that hotel brochure, but the one I remember seeing had a few out of focus shots. The ones that were in focus were the ones I remember Jaime focusing.

I never worked with Ren or Angela again.

Model Behavior

I was somewhat lucky in the timing of when I started in the modeling business. During the late '70s, drug use, particularly cocaine, was very common, with many models and photographers using it regularly.

By the time I started, that had slowed quite a bit, but there was still a lot of alcohol use and abuse. I knew of quite a few models, primarily men, who showed up on the set, drunk.

Some of them were good at masking the smell with mints, mouthwash, or cologne, but I could tell. I think the photographers and stylists could often tell, too. But, as long as the job turned out OK, nobody seemed too concerned.

These guys seemed to be OK as long as the job was not too long, and they were able to get a drink before and after the job, but if we were ever on the set for the majority of the day, where they couldn't get access to a drink, things went downhill.

I saw guys who would start sweating and shaking, signs that they had gone too long without alcohol. Sometimes, if they had recently had a little too much, they had a hard time standing up straight, and would sway a little.

One of the guys I felt the sorriest for, and one I liked the most, was a model named Austin. Austin and I had worked together a lot in Dallas, and we were with the same agencies.

We were in Osaka, Japan at the same time, and would often be at the agency office at about the same time each day. Usually, we would show up at the agency in the morning, on days we didn't already have a job booked.

One of the things that often surprises Americans, when I tell them about Japan, is that there are vending machines along the street, selling beer. Anybody, at any time, can walk up and buy various sizes of beer.

This was perfect for Austin. "Do you want to go get a beer?", Austin would ask me almost every single day. "It's 10:00 in the morning, Austin. No thanks.", I would protest. So, having done the polite thing, asking if I would join him, he would go off and have one (or two) anyway, by himself.

Austin died a few years ago of some sort of cancer. I would be very surprised if his drinking didn't play a major part in his early death.

Drinking by itself is a problem, but it also causes people to relax their discipline. For the women, and a surprisingly large number of men, this would lead to them eating more food than they could, and remain skinny enough for modeling.

Because of this, quite a few models adopted the binge-and-purge diet. It seemed to be the best of all worlds. Eat as much of anything you want, and not pay any price for it in your business.

There was a lot of self-delusion in models. There seemed to be the need to pretend that everything came easy, and that they didn't have to work at all at being thin and beautiful.

In reality, for most models, especially in my case, it was constant, hard work to keep in shape and be able to fit the clothes and look like what the clients wanted.

This pressure to appear to not work at things, while needing to look perfect, led to quite a few bizarre techniques. You remember Paul in Paris, who glued his ears back against his head? That was an example, but just the beginning.

With all the partying going on, morning bookings often brought the spectre of bags under the eyes to worry about. The women, in particular, would go to any length to get rid of the signs of excess. I knew a few women who actually used Preparation H (the hemorrhoid treatment) to reduce the swollen bags under their eyes. Since I don't see any of these women any more, I have no idea what the long-term effect this practice may have had.

And then there were just the plain old strange people. Every job has them, but in modeling, since you being a little different can actually help you, you have to do some really wacky things to get noticed. I'll give you four examples.

One of the models I met while in Osaka, Japan was Maria. Maria was an average model, probably never destined for supermodel status, and knew it. She was in it to have a good time and make a living for as long as she could.

Maria looked and acted pretty normal, except for one thing. She was obsessed with Rod Stewart. She carried a photograph of his mailbox in her wallet. Yes, the mailbox. She knew everything about him, everything about his music, and evidently, Rod's people knew everything about her, too.

Turns out, she had hung out a little too often at his house, and couldn't be seen there anymore.

Julie was in Japan at the same time at our agency. Julie was a very pretty model, who had been trained in ballet, but had grown too tall to be a professional.

Julie's obsession was with Bono of the group U2. She had been backstage a few times at concerts, and was convinced that her destiny was to be with Bono. Every little coincidence in life, she attributed to this undeniable future with the rock star.

For example, once when all of the models were watching a pro tennis match on television, Julie jumped up and screamed, "That's the guy! I knew it! I knew it! You see? He was at the concert. This proves I will be with Bono."

All of the guys just looked at each other, wondering if we should stay or run from the room. What she was talking about was, at an earlier concert, she sat next to this particular tennis pro, and met him backstage with Bono after a concert.

First of all, we reminded her that a lot of pretty girls get to go backstage, as do professional athletes. That should be no big cosmic event. But she was not deterred. She was convinced that there was a link between the fact that a pro tennis player was playing in a tournament on TV, being played in Japan, while she was in Japan. As far as I know, she never lost her belief that she will someday be with Bono.

Also in Osaka, Japan, was Susan. Susan was a male model trophy hunter. She would often take out and show us her collection of composite cards of men she had gone out with, and subsequently had been to bed with.

She appeared to have very little interest in a long-term relationship, and seemed to only be interested in adding more cards to her collection.

My last example is of a guy who either was really secure in his heterosexuality and just didn't care who thought what about him, or that he was able to live a dual life, living as a straight guy in the U.S. and as a gay man in Paris.

I had worked with Ed in Dallas and Paris, and he had worked into the market in Paris, seeming to get every job he auditioned for. It took a while for me to figure out how he did it.

The most influential guy in Paris at the time was an agent named Paul. Paul had taken Ed under his wing and had managed to get Ed major campaigns, ones that all of the guys in town had tried for.

The word on the street was that Ed was Paul's lover. I thought that was odd, since I knew Ed was married and had kids. Because of this reputation, Ed had access to the inner circle of the Paris fashion scene. He made a lot of money by being with the right people.

Whether Ed really was Paul's lover, or if he had just allowed the rumors to circulate to his advantage, no one will ever really know. Either way, it worked for him.

Character & Lifestyle Ads

There is one other major category of modeling left to discuss, with two subdivisions. I call them Character Models and/or Lifestyle Models. Basically, these are jobs that use "ordinary looking" people in ads. Sometimes the people are supposed to fade into the scenery, and other times they are supposed to evoke emotions or draw attention to the mood. Sometimes, they are supposed to be outrageous.

Japan department store ad

Usually, actors are cast for these types of ads. Photographers and creative directors want to make sure that the model can follow direction and fit the mood of the shot. Since fashion models are accustomed to bringing attention to themselves, actors are usually selected.

Ads that required action

Advertising agency executives, creative directors, photographers, or anybody who needs to get the right person for the right job, will reward the model who can perform exactly as requested. One photographer, who I tried to work with for years, when I finally was able to get cast for one of his photo shots and did well on the job, used me continually after that.

Professionals respect other professionals, and want to be around people who will do a good job.

That's A Wrap

I didn't grow up wanting to be a model or actor. I never even considered it until I was 25 years old. When I had reached a point in life where I was looking for a new challenge, and for a way to move into my own business, the opportunity to model presented itself to me.

Because I viewed it as a business, I was open to aspects of the business that other models and actors may have overlooked. Other models were so intent on getting fashion magazine covers or cosmetics contracts that they never explored the opportunities I tried. While I was trying for the same high fashion jobs all of the other models were fighting over, I also kept my options open and was able to make a good living, while the others had to wait tables or take other jobs.

Not only did I find opportunities (or they found me) in hand and parts modeling, runway modeling, voice overs, TV commercials, specialty advertising, and movie extra work, but I learned enough about myself during this period to have the confidence to go on to start my own businesses.

Primarily because of the confidence I gained in this first attempt at being my own boss, I went on to start several of my own business ventures, including an athletic clothing line, a head-cooling headwear system, a chain of retail vitamin stores, and my own line of nutritional supplements.

I stepped directly from modeling into my own business, doing a runway show for Neiman Marcus on a Thursday, to opening my own retail store on Friday.

The confidence and skill I gained from modeling, acting, and voice work helped me in many ways in my own businesses. I have regularly been called upon to speak in front of groups, appear on television and radio, and to be quoted in newspapers and magazines. I even had my own radio show for a couple of years.

I know quite a few models who went on to establish their own businesses, or work for other companies after their modeling years. One of the most common jobs that models seem to be best suited for is that of sales rep. Auditioning for modeling jobs or TV commercials was the best sales training I ever had, including professional sales training I received in a corporate setting. Being able to quickly assess the clients' needs, make the best presentation possible, and not take the results personally, are essential elements to both auditioning and sales.

If you are a model, or if you decide to get into modeling, pay attention on the job. If you study the business concepts, and the things that the professionals do on the job, you will be able to translate that learning into another job, should you not be one of the lucky few to make it to supermodel status.

There are a lot of ex-models in the world.

How-to Section Of The Book

About Hand/Parts Modeling

There are several things that a prospective hand model should do to get into and excel at the business. Here are some of them:

<u>Things to have with you on the job</u>—manicure kit, flesh-toned powder and/or makeup, glycerine and/or moisturizer, long sleeved shirts and jackets, appropriate jewelry. Learn how to make your hands look perfect, even if they don't normally. I used to bring a lupe (photographer's magnifying device) to see them up close and tight.

<u>Performance on the job</u>—Learning to move hands in small, deliberate increments. Learn to take direction and translate that into exactly what photographer/director wants. This is the most important thing to do to get future jobs. If the client knows that you will provide exactly what they want, quickly and accurately, they will save time and money with you.

<u>Difficult aspects of the job</u>—Getting rid of the rest of the body. When your hands are being photographed, the rest of your body is useless and in the way. You will regularly have to have curtains or stiff cards placed between you and your hands, making it impossible to see them. This makes it absolutely essential that you can listen to direction and make your hands do what is requested. This takes practice.

Misconceptions About Hand/ Parts Modeling

<u>Anybody can be a hand model</u>.

> While it is true that hand/parts models are often not what you would call fashion models, it never hurts to make yourself look your best. If you were the client, and two hand models came in for the audition, which would you choose, the average one or the attractive one? Many of my hand bookings came from previous fashion shoots, where someone noticed my hands. Likewise, I was booked for fashion jobs, as a direct result of someone noticing my overall look while on a hand photography set. Present the best package possible.

<u>You have to go to a professional manicurist to make your nails look good</u>.

> You can learn how to make your nails and skin look as good or better than a professional, for modeling shoots. Buy a good manicure kit. Learn what moisturizer or lotion makes your skin smooth. I used glycerine and applied it with cotton swabs. I knew a few women who were hand models who even slept with gloves on at night. I never went that far, but then I also had trouble sometimes covering up scratches from being a regular guy. Women can get more jobs in all types of modeling, including parts modeling, so it might be a good investment to take care of your hands.

<u>Hand/parts models don't have to prepare as much for jobs as fashion models</u>.

> While you don't have to sit in a chair and have your makeup and hair done for hours, it may take you as long to prepare your nails and skin to look good. Remember, all hand/parts by definition are closeups. I used a photographer's lupe (magnifying device used to view slides) to see what was going on close up. It may look strange, but you'll get more work when your hands never have any dry spots, split cuticles, or uneven white space under the nail.

<u>Hand/parts models don't have to worry about what they wear to the job.</u>

Professional hand/parts models usually have "brings", or items of clothing, jewelry, or accessories that the photographer may want you to have with you. It may be long sleeved shirts or jackets, watches, rings or anything that the client thinks makes their product look better.

Additionally, close up photography has specific requirements that other types of photography do not. You may be asked to wear black clothing to avoid reflecting the strobe, or there may a particular need for the job or client.

Try to wear comfortable clothing. You may be in awkward or uncomfortable positions for long periods of time, and you don't want your clothes to pinch or add to your discomfort.

How To Get Hand/Parts Modeling Jobs

With the exception of New York, it is extremely difficult to make a living with just parts modeling jobs. You can do it part time if you have a flexible regular job, but if you want to make a full time living at modeling, you will need to be involved in every aspect of the business possible. I did everything: fashion print modeling, commercial print modeling, industrial films, TV commercials, extra work for TV and movies, voice overs, AND parts.

After I had been a model for a year or so, a photographer asked me to do a "test shot" with him for a hand shot he had been thinking about doing. Test shots are unpaid jobs, in which a model and a photographer work jointly on a project intended to get them both more work in the future. Occasionally, the model is asked to split the actual costs of producing the finished product, but often the photographer gives the model a photo in exchange for his/her time on the project.

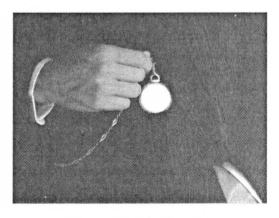

This was Mike's first hand job

This one photo, simply added to my regular model portfolio, led to a few hand bookings. As I accumulated more and more tearsheets (ads "torn" from magazines) of my hands, I decided to start a new, separate portfolio for hands and parts. I started listing "excellent hands" on my composite and agency headbook page.

Once I was making a significant portion of my income from parts, I went all the way, producing a parts portfolio, along with a combination portfolio of face and hands, and my regular fashion and commercial portfolios. I had a separate parts composite (calling card left with potential clients) printed, to go along with my standard, full body composite. When the agency printed its annual headbook, I bought pages in three separate sections; fashion, commercial, and parts. Every place it was an option, I listed my glove size, hat size, and ring size in my stats. Simply listing these stats tells potential clients that you are available for parts modeling.

Must-Dos To Be Taken Seriously In Hand/Parts Modeling

1. Build a portfolio of hands and parts photographs. As with all modeling portfolios, tearsheets of actual jobs are the best, but great photos showing your hands (or parts) in a variety of poses will show what you can do. Make sure that you have at least one photo clearly showing your face, not only to open up the possibility that you might get bookings that show your face, but also so that the client knows who you are when you walk in for your hand booking. I also recommend that you include at least one hand shot in your regular modeling portfolio, just in case.

2. Print a hands/parts composite. Be sure to include all of the necessary statistics on the card. For the same reasons mentioned above for the portfolio, it never hurts to have at least one photo showing both hands and face on your hands card. Again, it also is a good idea to add a hand shot to your regular modeling composite.

3. Buy a listing in the parts section of your agency's headbook. I recommend that you have pages in both parts, and fashion or commercial print, depending upon which category you best represent.

4. Keep hands/parts in great shape. A scratch can cost you not only this job, but other jobs with the same client in the future. Eat right, exercise regularly, get plenty of sleep, and take vitamin supplements, with emphasis on B-complex, Vitamin C, Vitamin E, Zinc, and Omega 3 oils (fish or flax). Ideally, you should never have to clip your nails. Filing nails regularly keeps them the proper length. Keep your hands moist and never let them dry out. This is hard in the winter, when lower humidity tends to cause lots of dry skin problems. Experiment with lotions, moisturizers, or glycerine to see which works best on your skin. Price is not a good gauge as to which will work best for you. Often, the lowest price product works as well or better than the higher priced ones.

5. Learn how to control movement. Steady hands get work the second time. Practice on a musical instrument or computer keyboard is a good way to simulate the motor skills needed for hand modeling. I have found that taking moderate amounts of Magnesium supplements can help to steady shaky hands.

6. Make a point of letting all your regular modeling clients know you do parts. Like any business, you must market yourself continually. This may mean going back through your client list and seeing each one again. This is not only essential to be able to get hand bookings, but also gives you a great excuse to remind those same clients that you do other types of modeling, while you're there.

How To Get An Agent

It takes a lot of work to get the right one, but you'll know it when you find it.

Because it is so hard to get full time work for parts, look for an agent that has a wide range of clients and types of work for its models. I don't know of any agencies, outside of one agency in New York City, that provide only parts models. I guess it's possible, but only in the biggest markets.

There are good ways to find agents, and there are bad ways. First, the bad ways. In my opinion, the internet is the last place to find an agent. Almost all "agencies" listed on the web are actually recruiting or scouting businesses, who charge models to be listed, with the promise that real agents are constantly looking for models on their site. Your hope, as a model, is that some big client will see your photos on this web site, and you'll become a star. Sorry, it doesn't happen that way.

The only good use for the web in finding an agent, is to look up the local agents in your town. The first thing you want to do is to weed out all of the escort services and peep shows that call themselves agencies. How do you do this? The only way is to call the agency's phone number listed on the web or in the phone book. The first warning sign is if you reach an answering machine or service. Hang up and move to the next one. When you reach a live body, ask if they take appointments for new talent or if they offer an open call each month. Write down the information provided and the name of the new talent director. Do this for all of the agencies you can find in your town. This will become important later.

The good ways to find an agent? One is word of mouth. If you know any models, ask them for the names of the top three to five agencies in town. You might find these names on your list that you made earlier, making them higher-ranking prospects.

The best way I know to find an agent, also adds a little marketing effort, but is a lot more work than most models want to do. I found that the models who work the hardest got the most work, so work as hard as you want to.

Look around you. In the newspaper, notice which local department stores run advertisements using models. When you're watching TV, do the same thing. Check out local magazines, direct mail, and billboards feature models in ads. Make a list of these companies.

Contact the companies on your list. If you need to visit their company websites, or look in the phone book, find the telephone number or email address to contact the company. Ask for the person who books the models for ads. Sometimes, you will be refered to an ad agency. Be persistent, you have nothing to lose at this point. When you reach the person who can tell you who books models, tell them what you are doing. Explain that you are getting into the modeling business and want their opinion on which agencies are the best. Ask them which agencies they think you should see.

This is doubly important. Not only will you be hearing straight from the "horse's mouth" about which agencies these clients actually use for models, you now have built a prospect list to call upon for jobs when you are ready with your portfolio. When you go back and schedule an interview ("go see") or are sent on an audition by your agent, you will have already established contact and have an advantage over other new models. You will already have something to talk about. You can thank them for helping you find your agent.

Compare all of the names that your sources have provided. Take the top three to five agencies, and schedule appointments with the appropriate person at each agency. See all of the agencies before you make a decision, even if the first one seems to be the "perfect" one. You'll know exactly which one is best, after meeting with them all.

Proceed With Caution When Looking For An Agent

No reputable agency will EVER require you to pay any money before agreeing to represent you. If you are asked to buy any packages of photos or other materials, or lessons, or anything that seems to link their representation to your money, walk away, and mark that agency off of your list.

There are legitimate reasons an agent may require you to spend money, AFTER they have agreed to represent you, and you are in. Some of those reasons are:

- **New or updated photos for portfolio**
  This may be especially true when moving into hands/parts.

- **New or updated composite card**
  Same as above.

- **Page in agency headbook** (annual)
  Ask a lot more questions if the agency asks for this immediately. While the timing of their headbook printing date may be entirely coincidental, this is a warning flag. There have been "agencies" that make their money from printing books, promising to have them sent to "all the major clients", but in reality, those books get thrown in the trash.

- **Incidental expenses** (courier fees for sending portfolios to clients, etc.)
  These should only be to recover actual expense, and should not charge the model more than the agency's actual cost.

Where to meet prospective agents

Never, ever, meet someone in a hotel room or any place that makes you feel uncomfortable. I don't know how many times I've seen "agents" or "art directors", claiming to be in town looking for new talent, call all the agencies in town and ask for a go-see, only to find out that they aren't what they represent themselves to be. They often are just getting their jollies by looking at pretty people, or maybe something more sinister. You just never know.

Only go to the regular place of business of an agency listed in the phone book. It should be in an office building or office/industrial complex, and not a residential neighborhood or obviously temporary setting.

If you ever get a weird feeling, turn and walk away. Do not worry that you will be missing some opportunity. Real opportunity in the business will come in nicer looking packages.

Not Getting Taken

The traditional way to become a model was to simply visit with an established agent, and either set up an individual appointment with the new talent director, or visit on their open-call day. Agents know exactly what types of people they will be able to put to work with their clients, and can give a thumbs-up or thumbs-down on the spot.

Many "experts" have cautioned new models that they should not have to pay for anything to get started in modeling. This is just not the case. Even legitimate agencies expect a model to build a professional portfolio, with photos taken by working photographers. Sure, your cousin's or next door neighbor's snapshots may be enough for the agent to identify you as an up-and-comer, but clients want to see professional work. Even models who have been working for years, still budget hundreds or thousands of dollars per year to update and upgrade their marketing materials. I don't know how many thousands of dollars I spent during my career, testing and printing photographs for my portfolio and composite cards. It was an investment in my business. Professionals in every type of business, continually put money back into their business, to grow it.

One term thrown around on modeling advice websites is that you should never have to pay for photos, but can do what is called TFP, or trade-for-prints. The reality of this is if you are already a working model, and a photographer wants to have you in his or her book, they might offer to give you photographs in exchange for spending an hour or two with them in their studio. This is often used to test new lighting techniques or new equipment, to add to the photographer's book, to get them more work. This is considered an investment in the photographer's book, and they cannot afford to spend time on a new model, helping them learn how to move or find the light. They want quality work from a professional model.

New models just can't get this type of arrangement for their portfolio photographs, particularly at the beginning, when they have no experience. Even if you have what the photographer considers to be an interesting look, they might be willing to offer to "test" with you, where you will be expected to pay the expenses, such as film and developing costs, and you get some photos in return. This is the most common way that models build their portfolio.

When you are brand new, you might even have to pay the photographer a session fee to get your "starter kit" portfolio photographs. This will be a nominal fee, usually lower than their regular session rate, and may range anywhere from a hundred dollars, up to two or three hundred dollars, plus the cost of any prints you request.

Since you need a portfolio that shows the range of work you can perform, you should include photographs from several different photographers. Professionals and clients can spot portfolios shot by one photographer immediately. You will get better and more frequent jobs if you have photographs from many sources, showing a wide range of the looks you can present.

There are now newer ways that people have employed to enter the modeling business. Modeling schools, modeling conventions, and talent scouting businesses promise that you will receive greater exposure from big clients by signing up with their service. Be very careful when you decide to try these methods. While some of them offer a decent value for the price you pay, sometimes providing all of the materials needed to get started at a reasonable price, there are quite a few unscrupulous individuals and groups out there, intent on taking your money, with no ability or intention to actually help you become a working model.

Here are some warning flags, when seeking help from schools, conventions, or scouting organizations.

The first is, how much are they charging?

- If you are paying more than a hundred dollars for each really good photo (look), that's too much.

- If you are offered only one photographer to shoot with, they have struck a deal with that photographer to receive a percentage of the photo session fee, and you will be paying too much for the photos.

- If they offer you a payment plan for your photos, they know that they are charging too much, and that the only way they can get people to join is to make the pain less intense with each payment.

The next warning flag is, who initiated the process?

- Did you see an ad in the newspaper for open calls or auditions?
- Did someone approach you at the mall and say, "You should be a model"?
- Did you hear that "all the major agencies" will be at a particular convention?
- And most importantly, is money required for you to be a part of their business?

Normally, prospective models decide that they want to get into the business, and contact the agent about representation. Agents tell you yes or no, based upon their professional opinion. Schools, conventions, and scouts change this process, and find you.

I don't want to cast all modeling schools, conventions, and scouting companies in with the bad players, but you need to be careful when dealing with these groups. Often, they play with your ego, telling you things that you want to hear, instead of the hard truth. The truth is if everybody could be a model, it wouldn't pay so well.

Don't let your ego empty your wallet.

Is Modeling Right For You?

The first thing you should consider before you get into modeling is, how badly do you want it? If you have always wanted to be a model or actor, and would do it even if you couldn't make a dime at it, nobody is going to be able to talk you out of it.

Just keep in mind, you will almost always have to have another source of income to support what will most likely be an expensive hobby.

The jobs you take to support yourself will require that you leave your weekdays open. This is why so many actors and models are waiters. You can make a decent living, working in restaurants or bars at night and on weekends, and still go to all of the auditions and jobs.

If you're lucky enough to have a trust fund, or still live at home on Mom and Dad's money, you may be able to play at modeling for a long time before you need to make money at it. There will always be some lucky people in this situation. If you're like me, you're not that lucky, and need to pay the bills with another job until the show biz checks start coming in.

Another reason to keep a regular job on the side is the irregularity of jobs and paychecks in modeling and acting. Even if you begin working regularly, your paychecks will not be predictable, and may be much farther apart than your bills. A good, steady income will help you relax and not look panicked on auditions.

One of the most important things you can learn to suceed in modeling and acting is, to not take it personally when someone else gets the job. Maybe the client wanted a blonde, and you're a brunette. Maybe they needed a white guy and a black guy, and you're Hispanic. You have to be able to go to each and every audition or go-see with a fresh approach. Give it your best shot, and then forget about it.

If you can't go back and face the same photographer or casting agent, time after time, after they have not chosen you in the past, and be able to be just as fresh as the first time, you don't belong in the business. You absolutely must learn how to take rejection.

You need to sit down and be honest with yourself. Do you want to be famous, or just make a good living in a fun business? A lot of things you will do to make yourself famous, may not pay well, and offer no real guarantee of success. I always voted for the paycheck, and hoped that the fame would come. In my case, thankfully for the purposes of the book, I didn't get the fame some people seek.

There will be people who will volunteer to do things for free, in the hopes that the exposure will be worth them donating their time. That's a gamble that rarely pays off, but each individual must make that decision.

And for you parents who want your kids to be in show business, you have a few things to consider. My first piece of advice is, always emphasize school over modeling/acting. Always.

Modeling and acting can be entered into, exited, and re-entered many times in life. School, on the other hand, is very difficult to restart, once you have stopped. So many things get in the way.

Many teenage girls talk their parents into letting them go to Europe to model. Many quit school after getting a magazine cover or two, and some never even finish high school, without that supermodel career they thought was surely coming.

When it comes to college, modeling and acting can actually coexist with acquiring an education. I knew quite a few models working their way through college. Many more had scholarships or parents paying their way to school, and were just modeling to make spending money. Both are viable paths to take.

My opinion is that school should always be the priority. Remember what I said earlier, that there are a lot of ex-models in the world. How often do you hear of twenty five year old ex-engineers or ex-lawyers?

The best advice I can offer to those considering getting into modeling and/or acting is, remember that it is a business to everybody else you will be working with. Make it a business, and you will learn to make money in it. Make it a hobby, and you will have fun at it. Make it a way to feed your ego, and you will get none of the above.

Working in modeling allowed me to see the world in ways not possible when just visiting on vacation. There are a lot of good things that can come out of modeling and acting, if you go into it with the right attitude and preparation, and having taken the proper precautions.

Whether or not you make a living in the business, go into it with the right mindset, and you will gain from it.

0-595-30894-5

Printed in the United States
17181LVS00005BA/256